Hello, Family Members,

Learning to read is one of the most important accomplishments of early childhood. **Hello Reader!** books are designed to help children become skilled readers who like to read. Beginning readers learn to read by remembering frequently used words like "the," "is," and "and"; by using phonics skills to decode new words; and by interpreting picture and text clues. These books provide both the stories children enjoy and the structure they need to read fluently and independently. Here are suggestions for helping your child *before, during,* and *after* reading:

Before
- Look at the cover and pictures and have your child predict what the story is about.
- Read the story to your child.
- Encourage your child to chime in with familiar words and phrases.
- Echo read with your child by reading a line first and having your child read it after you do.

During
- Have your child think about a word he or she does not recognize right away. Provide hints such as "Let's see if we know the sounds" and "Have we read other words like this one?"
- Encourage your child to use phonics skills to sound out new words.
- Provide the word for your child when more assistance is needed so that he or she does not struggle and the experience of reading with you is a positive one.
- Encourage your child to have fun by reading with a lot of expression . . . like an actor!

After
- Have your child keep lists of interesting and favorite words.
- Encourage your child to read the books over and over again. Have him or her read to brothers, sisters, grandparents, and even teddy bears. Repeated readings develop confidence in young readers.
- Talk about the stories. Ask and answer questions. Share ideas about the funniest and most interesting characters and events in the stories.

I do hope that you and your child enjoy this book.

—Francie Alexander
Reading Specialist,
Scholastic's Learning Ventures

For Guiseppe, Our Lively Maine Captain
— C.R. and P.R.

For Carly, Jennifer, and Evan
— C.S.

Special thanks to Laurie Roulston
of the Denver Museum of Natural History
for her expertise.

ISBN: 0-439-20635-9

Text copyright © 2001 by Connie and Peter Roop.
Illustrations copyright © 2001 by Carol Schwartz.

All rights reserved. Published by Scholastic Inc.
SCHOLASTIC, HELLO READER, CARTWHEEL BOOKS and associated logos
are trademarks and/or registered trademarks of Scholastic Inc.

Library of Congress Cataloging-in-Publication Data

Roop, Connie.
    Octopus under the sea / by Connie Roop and Peter Roop; illustrated by Carol Schwartz.
        p.   cm.— (Hello reader! Science. Level 1)
    ISBN 0-439-20635-9 (pb)
    1. Octopus—Juvenile literature. [1. Octopus.] I. Roop, Peter.
II. Schwartz, Carol, 1954- ill. III. Title. IV. Hello science reader! Level 1.

QL430.3.O2 R66 2001
594'.56—dc21

                                                                00-044543

20 19 18 17 16   6 7 8 / 0

Printed in the U.S.A.   23
First printing, May 2001

OCTOPUS UNDER THE SEA

by Connie and Peter Roop
Illustrated by Carol Schwartz

Hello Reader! Science — Level 1

SCHOLASTIC INC.
New York Toronto London Auckland Sydney
Mexico City New Delhi Hong Kong

Who lives under the deep blue sea?
Who has more arms than you or me?

An octopus!

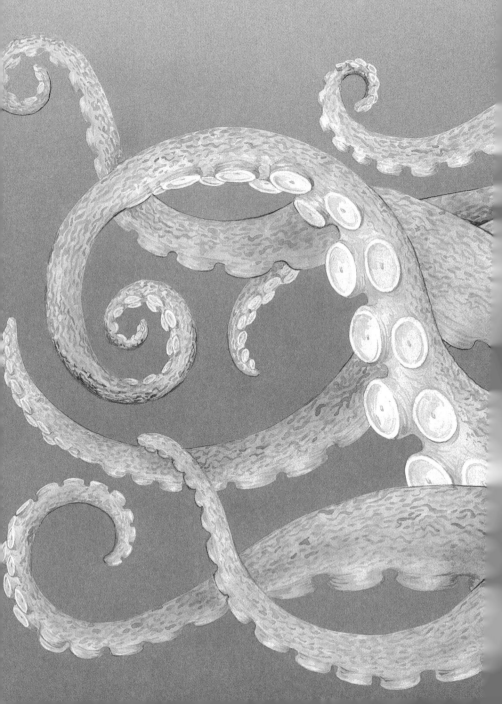

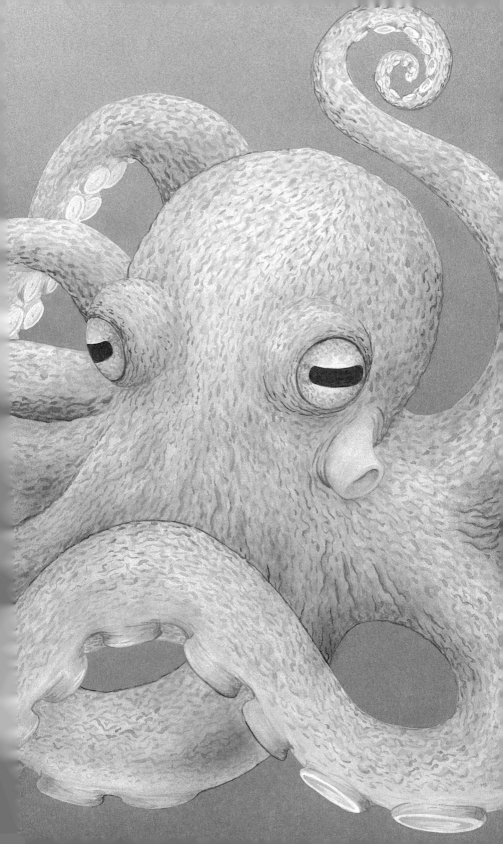

Long, long arms, eight in all,
help an octopus creep and crawl.

An octopus grabs its meal—
a crab, a shrimp, a tiny eel.

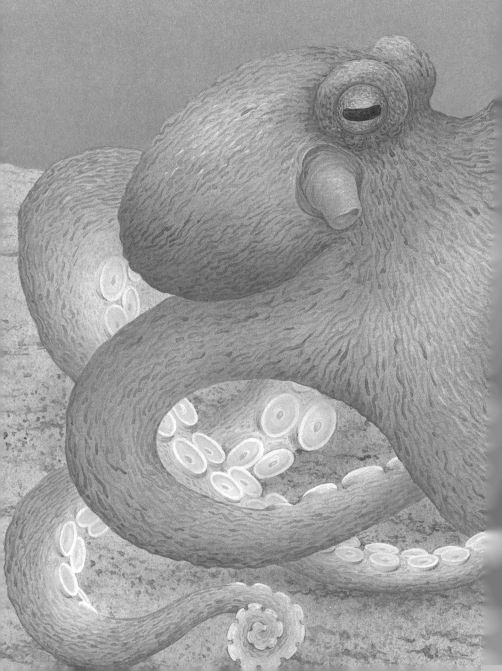

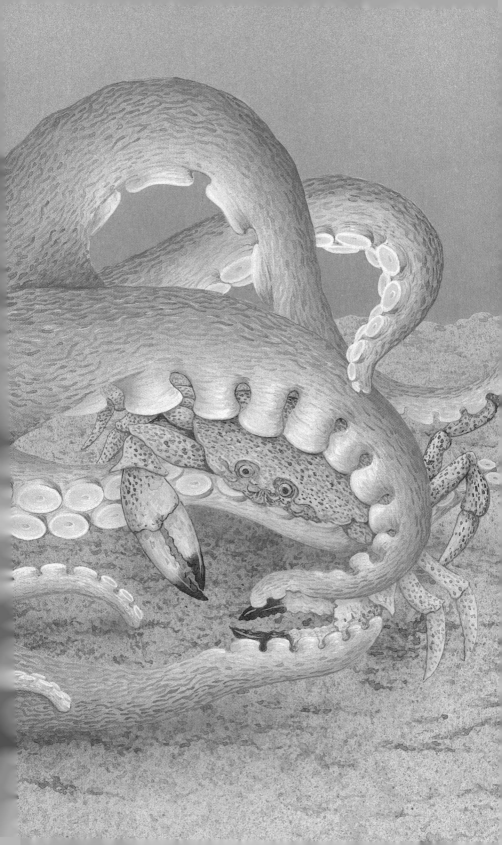

An octopus jets under the sea
by squirting out water so it can flee.

Hungry sharks and other fish
want a tasty octopus dish!

Look! As quick as you can blink,
an octopus shoots out dark, black ink.

This thick cloud is just a trick
so the octopus can escape...quick!

An octopus seems to disappear
when it knows danger is near.

An octopus has no bones
so it can squeeze into tiny homes.

These homes are holes, cracks, and caves far below the ocean waves.

A mother octopus, with her arms,
protects her eggs from any harm.

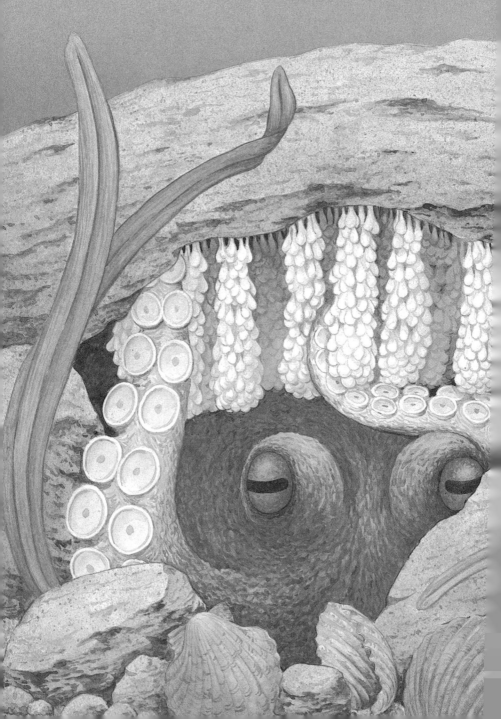

An octopus can be as long as a whale.

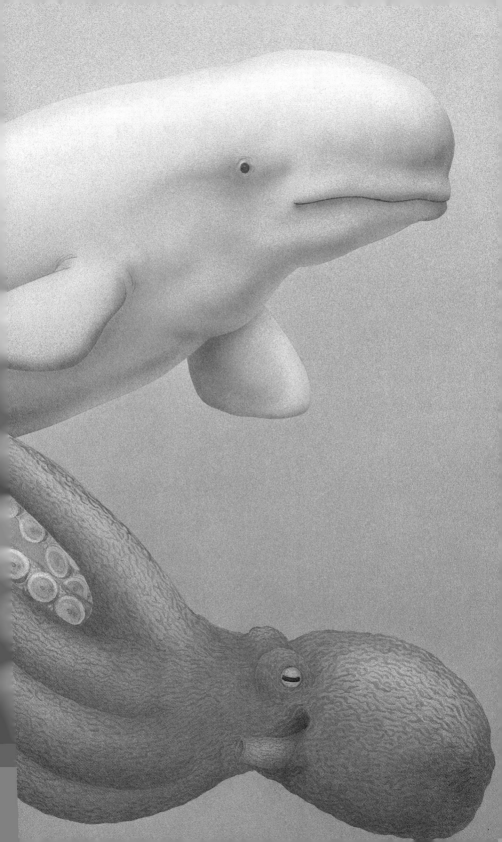

An octopus can be as small as a snail.

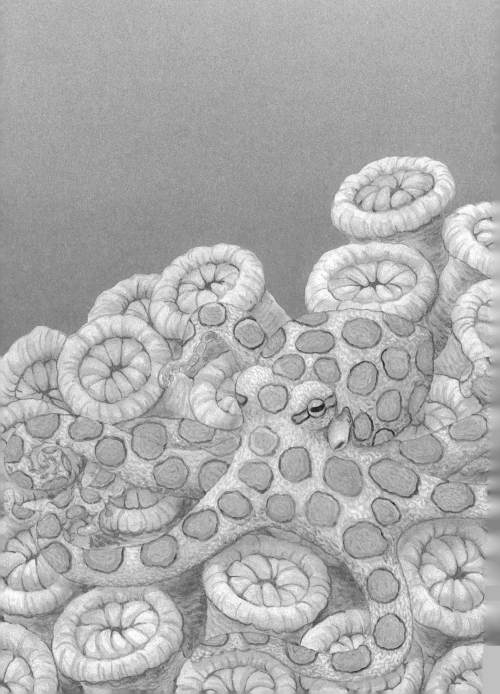

An octopus eats, hides, and flees
in every one of Earth's blue seas.